TCHAIKOVSKY- Very Best
for piano

Pyotr Ilyich Tchaikovsky
(1840-1893)

Catalog #07-2031

ISBN# 1-56922-068-9

EXCLUSIVELY DISTRIBUTED BY

CREATIVE CONCEPTS
P U B L I S H I N G

HAL•LEONARD®
CORPORATION

Visit Hal Leonard Online at
www.halleonard.com

Tchaikovsky in academic robes to receive an honorary doctorate of music at Cambridge University in June 1893.

TCHAIKOVSKY - Very Best for piano

Contents

A photograph of
Tchaikovsky
inscribed to
Valérie, wife of
Felix Mackar,
with a fragment of
the Andante
Cantabile from his
First String
Quartet of 1871.

ANDANTE CANTABILE
(Fifth Symphony) Opus 64

Pyotr Ilyich Tchaikovsky
(1840-1893)

ANDANTE CANTABILE
(Quartet) Opus 11

Pyotr Ilyich Tchaikovsky
(1840-1893)

Andante cantabile

18

ALBUM LEAF
Opus 19, No.3

Pyotr Ilyich Tchaikovsky
(1840-1893)

Allegretto simplice

ARAB DANCE
(From "Nutcracker Suite")

Pyotr Ilyich Tchaikovsky
(1840-1893)

Allegretto

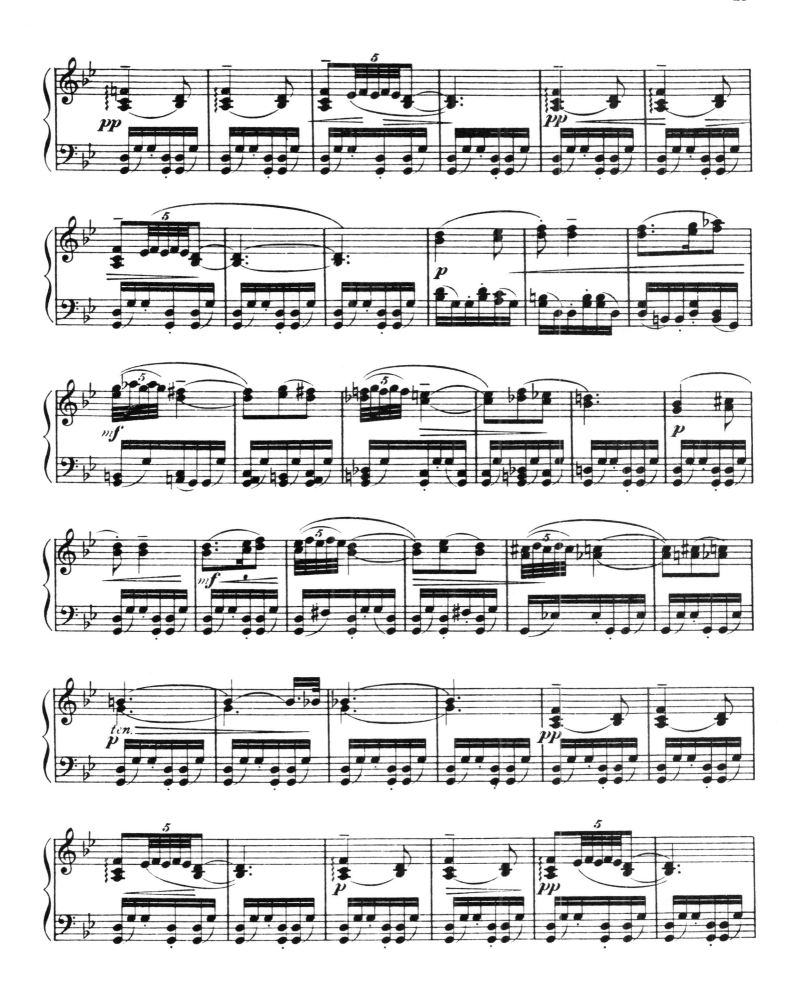

AT CHURCH
Opus 39, No.24

Pyotr Ilyich Tchaikovsky
(1840-1893)

CAPRICCIO
Opus 8

Pyotr Ilyich Tchaikovsky
(1840-1893)

Allegro giusto

Andante

molto espressivo

CHANSON TRISTE
Opus 40, No.2

Pyotr Ilyich Tchaikovsky
(1840-1893)

Allegro non troppo
la melodia con molto espressione

CHANT SANS PAROLES

Pyotr Ilyich Tchaikovsky
(1840-1893)

Allegretto grazioso e cantabile

DANCE OF THE REED FLUTES

(From "Nutcracker Suite")

Pyotr Ilyich Tchaikovsky
(1840-1893)

CONCERTO (Theme)
Opus 23

Pyotr Ilyich Tchaikovsky
(1840-1893)

1812 OVERTURE

Largo

Pyotr Ilyich Tchaikovsky
(1840-1893)

EUGENE ONEGIN
(Selected Themes)

Pyotr Ilyich Tchaikovsky
(1840-1893)

Molto espressivo (Lenski's Aria)

Tempo di Valse (Entr'acte Waltz)

GERMAN SONG

Pyotr Ilyich Tchaikovsky
(1840-1893)

ITALIAN SONG
Opus 39, No.15

Pyotr Ilyich Tchaikovsky
(1840-1893)

HUMORESQUE
Opus 10, No.2

Pyotr Ilyich Tchaikovsky
(1840-1893)

Allegretto

JUNE BARCAROLLE
Opus 37, No.6

Pyotr Ilyich Tchaikovsky
(1840-1893)

Andante cantabile

Poco più mosso

Tempo I

LARK'S SONG
Opus 39, No.22

Pyotr Ilyich Tchaikovsky
(1840-1893)

MAMMA
Opus 39

Pyotr Ilyich Tchaikovsky
(1840-1893)

Andante espressivo

MARCH OF THE TIN SOLDIERS
Opus 39

Pyotr Ilyich Tchaikovsky
(1840-1893)

Tempo di Marcia

MAZURKA
Opus 39, No.10

Pyotr Ilyich Tchaikovsky
(1840-1893)

MELODIE
Opus 42, No.3

Pyotr Ilyich Tchaikovsky
(1840-1893)

Andante con moto

MELODY IN A MINOR
Opus 40, No.6

Pyotr Ilyich Tchajkovsky
(1840-1893)

Allegretto

Ped. simile

MIDSUMMER REVERIE
Opus 37-A, No.7

Pyotr Ilyich Tchaikovsky
(1840-1893)

Allegro moderato con moto

MORNING PRAYER
Opus 39, No.1

Pyotr Ilyich Tchaikovsky
(1840-1893)

Andantino ($\quad$ = 66)

NEAPOLITAN DANCE

Pyotr Ilyich Tchaikovsky
(1840-1893)

Più mosso

NONE BUT THE LONELY HEART

Pyotr Ilyich Tchaikovsky
(1840-1893)

Andante ma non troppo

(The) ORGAN GRINDER

Pyotr Ilyich Tchaikovsky
(1840-1893)

Moderato

(The) NUTCRACKER
(Casse-Noisette)

Pyotr Ilyich Tchaikovsky
(1840-1893)

Allegro guisto (Miniature Overture)

Commodo (Arabian Dance)

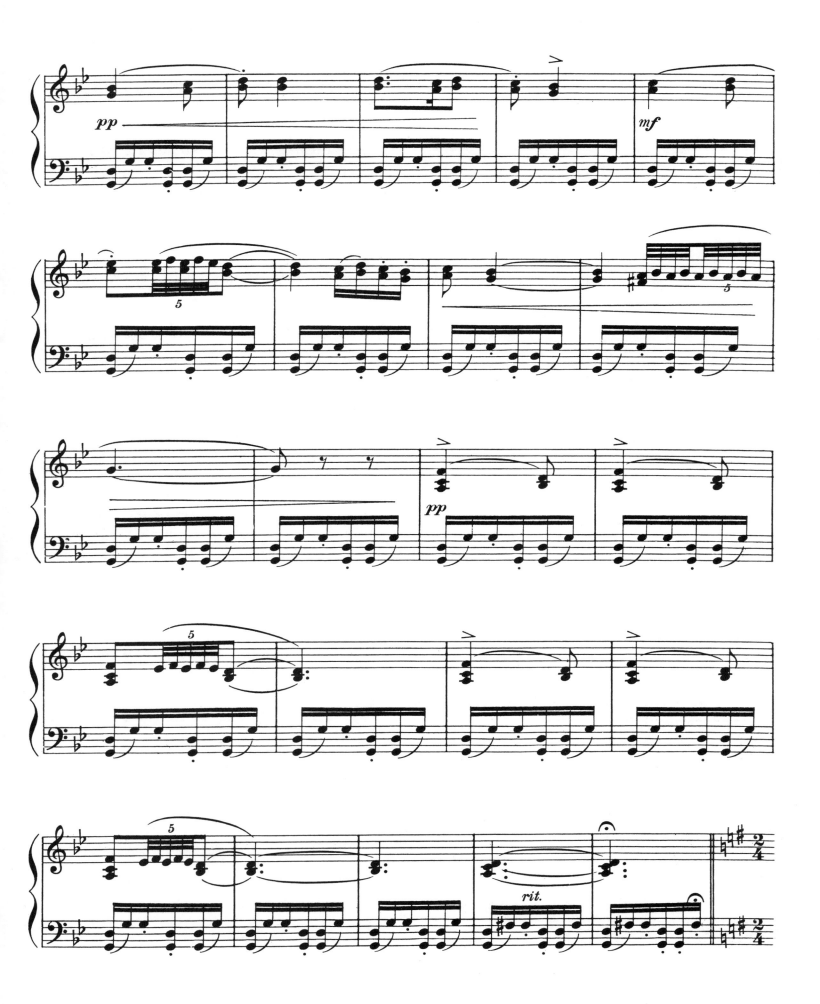

Molto vivace (Trepak)

(Valse des Fleurs)

ROMANCE
Opus 5

Pyotr Ilyich Tchaikovsky
(1840-1893)

RUSSIAN DANCE (Kamarinskaja)
Opus 39, No.13

Pyotr Ilyich Tchaikovsky
(1840-1893)

ROMEO AND JULIET
(Love Theme)

Pyotr Ilyich Tchaikovsky
(1840-1893)

Andante cantabile

SCHERZO
Opus 21, No.6

Pyotr Ilyich Tchaikovsky
(1840-1893)

Allegro vivace

Tempo I

SWAN LAKE BALLET
(Theme)

Andante

Pyotr Ilyich Tchaikovsky
(1840-1893)

SCHERZO A LA RUSSE
Opus 1, No.1

Pyotr Ilyich Tchaikovsky
(1840-1893)

Allegro moderato

SLEEPING BEAUTY

Pyotr Ilyich Tchaikovsky
(1840-1893)

To Coda ⊕

SONG WITHOUT WORDS
Opus 2, No.3

Pyotr Ilyich Tchaikovsky
(1840-1893)

SWEET DREAM
(Reverie)

Pyotr Ilyich Tchaikovsky
(1840-1893)

SYMPHONY NO. 6
("Pathetique")

Pyotr Ilyich Tchaikovsky
(1840-1893)

(A) SONG OF SADNESS
Opus 40, No.2

Pyotr Ilyich Tchaikovsky
(1840-1893)

Allegro non troppo (♩ = 112)
la melodia con molta espressione